Midnight Path

Choynika Hossain

BookLeaf Publishing

India | USA | UK

Presentation by *BookLeaf Publishing*

Web: www.bookleafpub.com

E-mail: info@bookleafpub.com

ISBN: 9789360948344

First edition 2024

This book is dedicated to Shane. Thank you for always inspiring me. I love you.

ACKNOWLEDGEMENT

I want to express my sincerest gratitude to Shane. His faith, love, and support in me have helped me to gather the courage to pursue my dreams. His presence in my life provides inspiring ideas from moments spent together. I would also like to thank friends and family for their presence and support in my life without which I would have no experiences to write about.

Zweihänder

Light gathers then scatters into space,
As the moon beams upon your face.
A lunar glow on each line carved by time.
Tempting me to draw your heart to mine.

This moment an illusion, my soul in collusion
to the heavenly hell lying beneath our feet
at war with the starry skies to which you speak
with your quiet stare, straight smile, and an
embrace.

A yellow star dusts your existence with grace
My fingers entangle with yours in faith
Shooting stars fall like fiery wraiths.
I wish upon them in hope, in search of escape
for just one moment, one minute, one hour of
wait
for the open arms of your soul accepting fate.

I gaze longingly at your face in the reflective
blade
One moment in time seared across its name
As I rise from my knees, Roman city in flames
I run into battle with your face ingrained
Across the German sword, you famed
Zweihänder.

You and Me

When we sat together at that picnic table,
I created fables of your blue eyes.
Fairytale endings of loving pretendings.
Beginning and ending with you and me.
Your knees collide with mine as we sit,
your guitar in your lap and mine in mine,
I distractedly think how well we would fit,
as your hands begin plucking the strings,
of that Led Zeppelin song your Mom,
inspired you to learn and sing.

My heart calls out for shaping,
my mind in chaos and destitute,
I have many words playing,
explaining, but I remain mute.
I do not express my love in fear,
you don't love me the way I love you.
I crave your mind, soul, and body.
Beside me, on me, forevermore.

Two Bicycles

Two bicycles ride in unison.
Wheels like great minds,
spinning revolutions.
Hands on the handlebars.
Handling the tension.
Of obstacles in our path,
while on a mission.
To go the distance.
With patience.
Heart racing
toward the journey.
The real destination.

Story Mountain

Wisdom peeled back from curtains of time
Watching a continuous playthrough of your
life.
Each chapter a mountain of rising actions
Each conflict's a lesson leading to climax,
An untapped and unreached part of me.
A story still unfolding not ending.

The Deepness Monster

Walkin' through a paved path.
Alone with nature, imagining that
waves are rising and falling one dark night.
In the vastness of the pond, to my right.

A chuckling voice suddenly roared.
The words drowned by flapping birds.
Animals flee in anticipation and in
discomposure.
Of the reemergence of the large creature.
Awakened from its slumber to meet its seeker.

A massive head surfaced with a watery snout.
Shiny, white teeth in its serpentine mouth.
Snake-like body with glistening, green scales.
Reeds and algae tumbling off its tail.

Bright, blue eyes turned to me and stared.
"Behold! I have arisen!" it said.
"The Deepness Monster wants to be fed!"
I watched in horror as the realization struck.

I am a meaty morsel, it's just my luck!
I hid behind a tree shaped like a twig.
A cackling raven picked me up, and threw me
in.

Water began rushing into the orifices of my
mouth.
I thought I would die when a tail whipped me
out,
launching me in the air landing me on the back
of the great beast, I clung on like a backpack.

In the next moment, it reared its head to me.
"Fear me not friend!" it said lovingly.
"We will ride the waves together."
"We will float on top until forever."
The beast ran its tongue on me soothingly.
I closed my eyes in that moment peacefully.

When I awakened, years after it kissed me
I sat cross-legged under a willow tree.
I realize, only now, that I've been set free.

Spirit

A creator of art and ingenuity.
A spirit of light and generosity.
Green pastures and windy
hills enraptured animals
as they jump joyously in
summer's green fields.

The days are long and
nights are warm as the
sun and moon rise and fall.

The tides of the moon
affect the lonesome walker
on the shores of the restless
waving water even as the sun
touches the sea, the colors of
life and its beauty would be nothing
if not for the eyes that can perceive,
the beginning and the end of days
and all that occurs in between.

Deadman's Float

I stand in the middle of a rising well.
Been here forever as far as I can tell
I stand here cold, wet, and defeated.
Torn, soiled clothes, nails embedded,
in the cracks of the cinder gray stones.
I crane my neck and squint my eyes
Through the round ring of white light
The exit and entrance so bright
The heavens wept right then
As the skies began to pour rain
In relieved exhaustion I sunk down
Into a pool of tears I feared I'd drown
Past my knees, past my torso,
I rest on my back in the water so
That my legs spring up to the top
My life force laboring on refusing to stop
Slow breathing, inflating my diaphragm
Laying with my eyes closed like a Deadman
As the rain drummed upon the world
The water filled the empty void of the dark
And I toppled over the edge of cinder blocks
Heaving, gasping, and thanking God
For the dark day and rain that pulled me
out.

Pages of Time

I sit on a green couch,
reading about writing
I turn the passages page by page.
Time slowly passes, slipping away.
The hour hand waves hello.
The second hand clicks its tongue.
The clock turns to face me
as time comes undone.
Words form minute after minute.
About the many seasons of life
In ways talked about before.
Experienced in other forms.

Hell's Door

Shaking hands rap at Hell's red flaming door.
Stumbling feet tripping asking for more.
The angels in the sky do not have what I seek.
I turn to the Morning Star in retribution for the
meek-minded souls of old who were not told of
death.
To be taken for nothing to suffer in stress.
Where are the miracles of power for gentleness?

Bruised arms and veins hungry for milksblood.
Dirty rubbers and burned spoons, what is left of
us?
Broken down to our knees praying for the weak
Chin up to heaven, hands as high as we can
reach.
Please forgive us for the tempting sins we seek!

Spilling tears and emptying cups of influences.
A world of right and wrong, black and white, no
nuances?
From beginning to end, the cycle of endlessness.

Caught in wave after wave of molten magma.

Where water meets flame, land will again form
us.
Starting over from birth, mankind will grow and
prosper.
Standing firm in love and goodness we will then
offer,
our souls to the never-ending needs of human
desire
We will yet again lose our souls to the eternal
fire.
Body and soul then burned to cinders in a
sinner's city.
Absent is God's voice, God why have you
forsaken me?

Love from Above

A pool of teardrops
That reflects mournful eyes
I tried to hide fears and regrets
By laying my aching head
on the crevice of your beating chest.

All your loving words
help fuel my healing.
They extinguish the
fire steering my mind.
When your healing hands
touch my body with love.
I remember everytime,
you were sent from above.

Mountain Lake

Undeniable hunger lusts beneath the surface
Of the perfectly still mountain lake
Blue fish swim in clear commotion
Not a single ripple forms in their wake
The mighty mountain's image is upon them.
All creatures tremble in their faces.
The heavens cry tears of survival
For all the creatures they must save
The mighty mountain carries its water
Down rivers of beauty and pain
Where it combines with the still mountain lake.

Midnight Passion

Closed eyes in the dead of night
Midnight dreams put up a fight
With iron bed sheets tightly wound
Around an iron will be too tightly strung
In deep recesses of a newfound
love unable to break away from
the feel of silky skin, two desperate
bodies inching into a fire rooted
between wordless lips and legs
Thighs parting as the heat kicks in
Two tongues touching, tasting as
One sinks into the other's salty sea
Both begin drowning in waves when
one head dips between the other's knees
Red delicate roses begin blooming
Even as their vases crash and fall
From two shapes entwined in loving
As their backs brace against the wall
Iron sheets turn into a castle,
within which two lovers unite,
in moments of beautiful passion
A dream becoming reality tonight.

Midnight

On dark summer evenings
As the sun sets on the horizon
As the yellow-orange beaming
sunlight fades, the night creatures
jolt awake. The midnight felines
strut in quiet padded steps over
noisy leaves and branches in their
way. The songbirds cease their singing
and retreat to their nests in the embrace
of boughs and owls begin looking for their prey.
 "Who?" They screech from their tree, "Who
will my next meal be?" Then mice scatter
and scurry from the beasts above
and the beasts below. Two creatures
in competition for, the satisfaction of
a full belly. Enticing mice are craved despite
their fear of losing a prey.
They know the night will give another day.
The owls and cats love the chase.
Feeding their souls by night before they lay.

Leave Your Mark

Two broken hearts walk into a bar,
to sit and talk about who they are.
Emptying cups to numb the pain.
Slurring words as they explain,
this was a chance encounter, not expected.
Love in the air, and their needs dictated
they drive down the street in his blue car.
Doubt and fears drowned by alcohol.
Driving any direction they choose.
Down memory lane, and dark alleyways
Either take me home or away from home.
You can decide where to park,
One way or another, you left your Mark.

Geppeto's Song

Upon Geppeto's balcony
wooden.

Up a winding Stairway
to Heaven.

A smokey afternoon breeze is
bringing,

A Led Zeppelin song a guitar is
singing.

New Beginnings

I know this man who used to sing
Mournful rap songs that would bring
Tears to the eyes of his future lover
His past was sad and kept undercover

He was told hopeful lies and he was
scorned
By women in his life who have torn
His heart to shreds but he never spoke ill
Of people from his past because he was still
A beautiful soul despite his pain from love
A heart as pure and good as a dove

My soul aches day after day to see him soar
I want every part of him like no one before
My fear and his fear are one and the same
We fear falling in love with someone again.

Grounded

On this desolate battlefield
With no signs of life,
I stand on the sterile earth
Chin lifted toward the sky
Eyes touching the place where the sky
And the ground meet
That is where I live.
Under the dome
Above the dirt.

Gray Spring

Gray light is cast upon
A normally sunlit day
As the sun hides behind
a weighted blanket,
heavy clouds bring rain.
Though the clouds cry in the sun's
absence, the pain in the skies is
nothing new. The rain washes away
the dirt and the sunlight shines anew
the dew drops on life emerging,
from the seeds of hope planted by love.
In the season of spring and growing
The sun and the rain create the garden's glow.

Dead Roses

I bought myself red, dead roses
Cut from a living bush with thorns.
I envisioned them in my room,
to fill the dark, lonely void.
If no one else is here,
I'll paint the town red.
I'll make my heart beautiful
Even if the roses are dead.

All In

Your presence is felt
in long absences
and long distances
and long silences.
An unspoken bond
Felt even in still lakes.
No matter how quiet your waters
I'll wade into the rippling circles
left in your wake.

Sweet Dreams

Show me something sweet
To make the night easy-going.
You lay sound asleep.
While the moon above is glowing.
So at peace is your face.
Your breath catches air.
Nose whistling through space.
You dream of landing and standing
upon wooden walls and rising decks
upon which the Milky Way gazes
at your life lived at the border
of your consciousness.

www.ingramcontent.com/pod-product-compliance
Lightning Source LLC
LaVergne TN
LVHW010259210726
843508LV00020B/2909